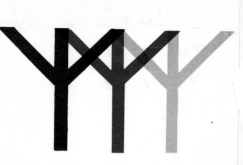

modern
art
in
flower
arrangement

Other Books by
Emma Hodkinson Cyphers

MODERN ART

in

FLOWER ARRANGEMENT

By EMMA HODKINSON CYPHERS

NEW YORK • HEARTHSIDE PRESS, INCORPORATED

Copyright 1959 by Emma Hodkinson Cyphers
Library of Congress Catalog Card Number 59-7985
Printed in the United States of America

Contents

modern

art

in

flower

arrangement

1 Willingness to experiment with new materials is one of the marks of the modern artist. Here a stabile on an aluminum turntable planned as "design for tomorrow" is titled *Showcase*. Flowers and artificial grapes in a "case" of clear plexiglass panels proportionately related and standing at right angles to one another produce a unique composition. The transparency creates an element of fluid space. *Arranger Mrs. John E. Everett—Photographer: Bryan Studio.*

PREFACE

A totally different style of floral design is appearing today in the flower arrangement world. Arrangers are experiencing one of those rare intervals in history when a change in art occurs to produce a new culture. This change is given various names but the term "modern" has general acceptance for none better designates an art-style suited to this age in which we live —an epoch marked by changing attitudes, changing customs, and changing aspirations.

Prompted by social, political, and economical environment, this modern movement is one of natural growth. To the artist who recognizes the signposts of change and has the foresight to follow them is offered opportunity to express himself freed from conventional techniques. A consequence is that the artist expresses his ideas in the way that suits his need best, even though he may not be easily understood.

Modern art has existed for a long time but we find it still requires a great deal of explaining. Viewers are often disturbed to the point of challenge and belittle the genuine character of the truly modern. This fact, however, does not declare the artist at fault. It may be that hostility is aroused because the artist's work confronts us with an entirely new experience. Every one has the right to question, of course, but let him question himself as well as the artist. If one claims he understands the work of the Old Masters but not the New, it is probable he doesn't understand *any* art, for the change that has come with the modern is only a bright new cloak for those fundamentals upon which all art is based; although principles may vary in emphasis, they never change.

This book is offered in an attempt to establish the place and influence of modern art in flower arrangement. Admittedly one notices a sentimental prejudice against it, a raising of the eyebrows as it were. This is a familiar pattern for throughout the ages new developments have confused and puzzled the public.

However, since in any age of experimentation, and such is the twentieth century, it is the designer who decides the style of his work, and since in creative art there is no set pattern, there should be no lifted eyebrows in response to an arrangement simply because it happens not to follow well-known standards. This is assuming the designer has kept within bounds of good taste, of course. I attach extreme importance to good taste. Just what this is defies definition, but in all attempts to describe this elusive quality, a common denominator *time and place* which is allied to the fitness of things, is to be found. Take, for instance, a color scheme startling to the point

of eye irritation were it looked upon any length of time. Such a plan befits a poster advertisement which is designed to attract attention; no one would declare this in bad taste. The same plan, however, in a bedroom is not inducive to sleep which is the purpose of the room, and so is in poor taste. This is an exaggerated example to be sure, but it makes meaning clear.

Perhaps the raised eyebrows have been prompted by the bizarre arrangement that occasionally meets the eye. Such work is untrue to our medium which in itself is beauty, and so in arrangement is a first requirement. But alas! In arrangement as in other fields of art, some results are grotesque. An abuse of liberty in expression contributes nothing to our art but is, I believe, a natural price to pay for freedom. Without doubt some of the arrangements displayed in the name of "modern" are products of a defiant attitude, but for the most part they represent nothing more than an undisciplined enthusiasm to be different! Voltaire aptly said, "We must be original without being bizarre." But even if the arranger fails in this respect, it is rewarding to see him explore new ideas. A big failure is better any day than a small success!

In spite of the occasional failure, the modern concept is a credit to the art of arrangement, as illustrations in this book reveal. Each is a structure whose quality is the product of the discernment, good taste, and skillful technique of the creator. Fundamental principles have supplied the basis for pleasing organization of ideas and materials. Modern approach has been fulfilled in direct proportion to the arranger's intended purpose and to the degree of stimulation he arouses in the beholder. True art, let it be remembered, is communication between the artist and the viewer, even if the message holds no more than an invitation "to see this striking color or these unusual forms." An aspiration on the part of arrangers toward greater communication through self-expressiveness, thereby producing a closer link between his work and the observer, is a most commendable development of recent years. It is one that definitely extends our work into the modern realm where the merging of expressiveness with design is a hallmark.

2 This bold, starkly simple design is achieved with just two elements. The self-sufficient branch tip of magnolia, in satisfying poise with the easy-on-the-eye, sweeping curve of driftwood, results in an arrangement which is complete and unified. In a gray-green ceramic (a Bee Basch original), on a slate-topped chest, this design is true to its time, its place, and its purpose. *Arranger: Mrs. Saul J. Shapiro—Photographer: Mrs. E. Stout.*

1

What is Modern Art?

Modern art is not without good firm roots for, contrary to common opinion, modern designers have not ignored the heritage of the past. The entire history of art is their concern and furnishes inspiration. In the realm of painting, for instance, Franz Marc borrowed from prehistoric art; Modigliani from Gothic sculpture; Roualt from Coptic textiles and the stained glass of the medieval era. The Cubists were influenced by the distortion and simplification of African sculpture while most of the Impressionists were inspired by the exquisite subtlety in the decorative design of Japanese prints. Persian painting intrigued Matisse; canvases of seventeenth century Spanish artists stimulated Monet. The art of Egypt and the South Sea Islands is evident in the work of Gauguin. Naive peasant designs and the simple art of primitive people motivated German Expressionists.

Borrowings from the past can be traced in all fields of art, but the modern artist, instead of imitating the original source of inspiration, has used it simply for direction and guidance. His vision is not bound to previous impressions of the subject; his own first impression is of greater import.

Not all contemporary artists are

3 The appeal of this design is visual—derived from the artist's awareness of inherent beauty in the large dry leaf. Combined with a palm spathe, trumpet vine pods, and glycerinized magnolia leaves, the structure has clean-cut delineation, interests the viewer's eye in itself and does not depend on memory or nostalgia to give it pleasure. *Arranger: Mrs. Paul Kincaid—Photographer: Sam Robinson.*

modern, for many follow old patterns and styles of art without sparking them with any degree of creative originality or freshening them through materials or techniques new to today's designers. With this in mind it is amazing and revealing to discover many likenesses to works of antiquity in the most modern of designs—or is it that many ancient patterns look modern?

ENVIRONMENT AFFECTS CHANGE

Modern work differs from the conventional because it is nurtured by a completely different point of view. Ours is surely the *space age* with interest in a new conception of space. Techniques in handling materials and the use of materials for their intrinsic character inspire us to integrate space in design so that it is as important as mass. (This principle applied to arrangement is shown in Plates 1 and 2). This is of more concern to modern artists than meaning or relation to the background in which it was designed.

If it is agreed that today's living conditions and opportunities supply environment for the growth of change, it is well to examine a few of the characteristics disciples of modern art are considering. A prominent feature is *speed;* surely we live in an age of speed. Hurried lives have led to informality, with pomp and ceremony of a former day giving way to entertainment

and excitement at the expense of repose and tranquility. The result is *complexity* in modern life. In answer to a resultant need for simplification, industry has reduced motor cars, airplanes, locomotives, furniture, accessories—even vases! —to simple forms.

Our age is strong in *dynamic quality* where nothing is permanent . Yesterday we were content to travel about on the ground—today we move in space. Yesterday we were satisfied to explore the earth— today man investigates formidable depths of the sea, and is making plans to reach the moon.

And *reason* too is a factor. To assure smooth association with individuals and with groups, people study psychiatry and sociology. Science and economics bring a broader knowledge and a desire for experimentation.

Machines have replaced hand labor, encouraging mass production as an economy measure and an incentive for constant change with products quickly becoming obsolete. This creates new desires and requirements. We have untold resources, countless new materials and processes to stimulate imagination and in the end, material progress.

RESULTS OF CHANGE

No intelligent person can afford to be unaware of the continuous evolution in the "great change." However, though it is apparent

4 While the design pattern and material (palm boots, eucalyptus, and a heavy poinciana pod) are predominantly circular, the arranger has introduced forceful contrasts (strelitzia) which compel the eye to move back into space and then back into the composition. Such strong contrast of color, texture, line, form and plane is pronouncedly modern. *Arranger: Mrs. Eric H. Feasy—Photographer: Russell Lawrence Young.*

that modern art coincides with progress in modern living, it should be emphasized that *change in art* is not necessarily *progress* in the field. Nor does it produce artistic work more "perfect" than the old school. It is just more "effective" since it more truly conforms to current urge. A logical view to take is that the place and significance of the modern movement in art is very real and very sound. When design leads to new styles arising from new materials, new needs, new wants, new problems, new opportunities for looking at things, and so new ideas, it is a growing art, not a fad.

CHARACTERISTICS OF MODERN

When we try to deduce a genuine style in modern art, we see first of all that it is designed with authority and is primarily concerned with aesthetic freedom and experimentation. Plates 3, 4, and 5 are illustrative. Modern art can best be summed up by a listing of its most pronounced characteristics which will be described in detail as the text progresses. In capsule form they are as follows:

In structure there is
    simplicity
    geometric factor
    clean-cut delineation
    bold design
    contrast in color, texture, line, form, and plane
    balance through tension equilibrium

    smooth or staccato rhythms
    space integration within compact composition
    occasional distortion
In color there is tendency toward
    earthy tones
    bold hues
    effects of sparkle
    use structurally, decoratively, symbolically, expressively
Texture
    takes the place of ornamentation
    is not considered separately but as integral part of the total effect
In content
    animation is dominant
    materials are used for their own beauty and individual expressiveness
    structural aids are exposed rather than hidden
    there is wide use of natural materials such as wood, metal, wrought iron
    there is use of new materials offered by industry such as cork, plastics, and others

In analyzing the plates you will note to what extent arrangers have incorporated these modern traits into their work. Some have been given greater emphasis than others, for individual talents move in different directions to produce diversity that is inevitable and desirable. The concepts, we can say, are as different roots of the same plant which taken collectively reflect the modern spirit. All are free of triteness which has stultified many arrangements of the past.

5 Solid planes of green dracaena leaves point up the delicate blue iris, producing a composition as modern as abstract sculpture. Rolled leaves play bulge against hollow to create strong form. Three transparent slabs—two standing upright with fern pressed between—are employed with a spirit of experimentation. *Arranger: Mrs. Eric H. Feasy—Photographer: Russell Lawrence Young.*

2

Survey of the Modern Movement

There is no better way to an enlightened understanding of modern trends in art than to draw upon the past; the very core of the subject is its general background.

In the brief and simplified outline to follow, only the precursors or founders of a particular group, or innovators in certain techniques, or the most influential supporters will be referred to; there are many others who might well be mentioned if space permitted. The work of those singled out, however, is enough to give a fairly accurate and conclusive description of the characteristics listed on the preceding page.

Our first examples are taken from the painter's realm. Books on the best-seller lists, motion picture and television productions have so publicized this aspect of art that it is more or less familiar to the layman.

Just what year marks the change is not important, for more significant than *when* is *why*. Then too remember that change is not a single happening—it is an evolution. But approximating the time in history, and thereby understanding the pulse and temperment of the populace, helps us to understand the movement.

MILESTONES IN THE MODERN MOVEMENT

If, as many claim, it is a *com-*

plete break with traditional power that determines when the new pattern began to emerge, the early twentieth century is the marker. At this time European painters stormed against aesthetic and social standards to such extent that rebellion spread throughout the world.

But the breath of a new spirit is traceable to earlier tendencies and prompts its inclusion in this brief survey. The French artist, Edouard Manet, severed conventional ties when he took disturbing license in painting the female figure. His half reclining *Olympia* nude (1865), startled the mid-nineteenth century public and it can be said certainly that he initiated the impulse toward expressive freedom. Nudes had always been idealized in art, but here was *realism* expressed by one who dared to make his model *real,* and the masses were aghast.

REBELLION AGAINST REALISM

The bitter condemnation of the realism of Manet challenged a group of young painters and influenced another rebellion which came to be known as *Impressionism.*

Also a strong influence in Impressionism was the Japanese print craze of 1853 which came about by accident. A shipment of crockery from the Orient, with Japanese prints used for packing, excited such interest that a Paris shop imported an assortment of the prints.

Artists frequently assembled there, prized them for their exquisite subtlety. In comparison, representation of nature by European artists semed dull and lifeless. The fresh color tones and the decorative proportions of light and dark areas in Japanese technique brought protest against the realistic likeness that absorbed Western painting at the time.

IMPRESSIONISM

From 1870 to 1890, Impressionism flowered as one of the strongest revolutions in art. Painting in the open air, these artists were linked in a common desire to depict atmosphere—particularly sunlight. This they did by means of "broken" color, an intermingling of little bits of differing hues. To paint the brightness of grass as they saw it in a sunlit atmosphere, for example, the Impressionists used dabs of yellow pigment beside dabs of green which the eye blended into a sparkling yellow-green. Applying pigment in this manner tended to break up form contour, turning art toward the beginning of abstraction. Even so, depicting quick visual impressions of objects rather than clarity of shape extended the visual experience of *realism*.

It can be said that Impressionism grew out of reality, for actually it was a kind of reality in which the artist caught a momentary aspect of nature. Claude Monet, for instance, as one of the greatest artists in this revolution, was concerned with light which diffused shapes, with light vibrations, and with the appearance of color from a distance. Thus he was led to paint a series of canvases displaying a haystack as he saw it under ever-changing light of the day. Plate 6. There were Edgar Degas with his revelation that shadows were composed of color, and Camille Pissarro with his division of color into primary components juxtaposed in small areas which caused the eye to recompose them into rich and varied tones to evoke emotion. How was this done? Instead of painting green with green pigment, for example, he used contrasting yellow and blue side by side so the eye would blend them into a more luminous green. Pierre Renoir used color almost as a mirror held up to nature suggesting fog, rain, wind, and other fleeting moments out of time. Originality thrived in this atmosphere of Impressionism. We might say that with this break with tradition came the desire to experiment, a concept in art which still motivates work today.

POST-IMPRESSIONISM

Near the close of the century a group of Impressionist adherents began to rebel against this art style. History reveals that these early moderns seriously studied the works of Old Masters in the Louvre, for in them they saw underlying structure and personal ex-pressiveness which was absent in the realistic paintings prominent at the time.

It is worthwhile to examine great masterpieces from the past to discover for yourself the emphasis on design which is a strong tie between the modern and the great art of the past. To do this, place tracing paper over a selected reproduction—I suggest *Madonna of the Chair* by Raphael—and trace the contour lines that define the light and dark areas. Now turn the tracing upside down to reveal a more or less abstract design and you will see one quite apart from the subject of the painting and interesting in itself.

From the most dominant of these post-Impressionist independents, the Frenchmen, Paul Cezanne and Paul Gauguin, and the Dutchman, Vincent van Gogh, stem the main forces of twentieth century art styles—*Abstraction* with emphasis on design, and *Expressionism* with emphasis on personal emotion. In these we find a return to a concern for surface design, and a personal expressiveness exactly opposite to Impressionism which never explored beneath the surface of a subject.

INTELLECTUALIZED ABSTRACT STYLES

The camera had been invented in the middle of the nineteenth century. A growing popularity in photography challenged an accepted viewpoint. No longer need a painter record physical likeness; the camera, except for color, could do it better!

Cezanne was faithful to the Impressionists' open-air painting, but he explored the more solid in nature. He influenced young artists to get to the *heart* of a subject and leave surface identity to the comparatively new device; thus was created a decorative and emotional aspect as opposed to the sentimental and representational view which had dominated the field of painting prior to this time. Again the eye was seeing in a new way. Cezanne's *Pines and Rocks* in its pattern of straight lines and angles with an illusion of depth through color, illustrates his thinking in terms of structure. In the matter of perspective, the eye moves around his canvas—not from just one point as had been practiced by earlier painters.

Cezanne's search for form made him a central figure among the post-Impressionists. In fact, his influence has been so great that the modern period in art is often referred to as "since Cezanne" with Cezanne himself called "father of modern art." His reaction against the "structural weakness" resulting from the Impressionist idea of things appearing rather vaguely in diffused light gave the art world his dominant contribution—analysis of nature's structure into basic forms of the cylinder, the cone, and the sphere. He achieved clarity of form to arrive at strength of structure as opposed to the indefinite contours of Impressionism. In his *Mont Sainte-Victoire* themes, the mountain is a cone, the houses are cubes, and the trunks of trees are cylinders with leafy masses painted in abstract shapes. Here is the forerunner of Cubism and all the abstract "isms" of the twentieth century.

In color Cezanne "molded" with the physical reaction of receding and advancing hues, a color theory in line with scientific optical dis-

6 (Opposite) To echo the blues and violets of Monet's *Belle Isle Sunshine* in arrangement, translucent fluorite set on two slabs of Italian marble, and. grayish blue-green spiralled eucalyptus, gray graptopetalum, and green hartstongue fern are accented by the reddish tone of Rex begonia and galax foliage. Texture contrast is noteworthy. *Arranger: Mrs. Dorst Baumgartner—Photographer: The Tampa Tribune.*

covery. On the principle that color near you appears warm, and distant cool, a sense of space was effected—a totally new handling of color inspired by the spirit of experimentation.

CUBISM

With the growth of modern art, experimentation continues to absorb artists. Perhaps it reaches the high point in Cubism. With Georges Braque and Pablo Picasso, the Cubist insurrection began early in the 1900's to become a definite facet in modern art. Artists were preoccupied with organizing space with the interrelationship of component abstract parts. The Cubist painter had no desire to imitate. A pioneer canvas was Picasso's *Les Demoiselles d'Avignon*, a pattern of zigzag lines and angled planes.

Another point of significance in the Picasso painting is the apparent influence of African Negro art in two of five figures. This art of a primitive people was brought into France by European conquerers of West Africa. The Paris art world became enthused over the economy of form and distortions of the Negro sculptures and masks which, we find, were to have great impact on twentieth century art. Primitive sculptures inspired the work in Plates 7 and 8.

Cubism passed through a variety of phases in which the external object was attacked. Shapes of a model or scene were overlapped, flattened out, and juxtaposed to show every static aspect (Plate 9); forms were broken up and reassembled into non-representational shapes (Plate 10).

This manner of seeing brought a new concern for texture which led to a technique called *collage*. In earlier work areas of textural variation had been incorporated into design for the sake of variety, but now texture becomes the picture, so to speak. In the collage, textures were achieved by mechanical means with foreign materials such as bits of cloth, thin strips of wood, and pieces of paper added to the painted surfaces. Relationship was incongruous but the finished picture was symbolic. An interesting example is *Grandmother* by Arthur Dove. With a page from a Bible, a piece of faded embroidery, pressed ferns, and weathered shingles the artist suggested grandmother's religious fidelity, age, patience, and fragility. Collage adapted to arrangement is seen in Plates 11 and 12.

Picasso is especially famed for his "two-faced" figures suggesting space from more than one vantage point. Here is a new wedge in relationship of things to correspond with Einstein's theory of relativity in which time is mathematically considered a fourth dimension.[*]

_____
[*]See **Design and Depth in Flower Arrangement**, published by Hearthside Press, Inc.

7 A cluster of abrus pods with black-spotted scarlet seeds familiarly known as "crab eyes," and dried
   cut palm are combined in a stylized design inspired by the strength and form of a primitive
   sculpture which like the palm is not a true copy of nature. *Arranger: Mrs. Howard M. Oberlin—*
   Photographer: Howard M. Oberlin.

8   The primitive distortion and simplification of a teakwood figure inspired this design. Bronze
chrysanthemums echo the color of the figure, the strelitzia repeats that of the Bali pottery bowl.
Novel utilization of space is seen in the broom knotted to repeat the shape of the bowl's handle.
The base is an inverted tray of monkey-pod wood. *Arranger: Mrs. Edgar Littmann—Photographer:
Eugene Taylor.*

9 With plant material "broken up and reassembled" according to the artist's personal pleasure, we find here a kind of abstraction that tends towards mysticism rather than geometry. There is mastery of design in the combination of orchid leaves, dried gladiolus foliage, coconut calyxes, in a container of palm fronds which are put together and secured upright in a maghogany block. A wooden Danish monkey completes this design in earthy tones. *Arranger: Mrs. Harry C. Groome, Jr.—Photographer: John Hugelmeyer.*

10   This represents another process of abstracting (taking apart and redesigning), with polished roots
     featured on a free-form base. The roundness of their curves organizes space in pleasing proportionate
     relationship. Placement of materials achieves three-plane relationship and indicates construction in
     deep space. *Arranger: Mrs. Robert Godley—Photographer: Mrs. Fred Langford.*

11 This charming screen, a space divided in the arranger's home, is based on the principle of the collage. Plant materials are flattened between two pieces of lucite, one opaque, one clear. *Arranger: Mrs. Edgar Littmann—Photographer: Eugene Taylor.*

Here, space is thought of as a kind of "time" shown simultaneously (Plates 1, 13). In Plate 13 curves appeal rather than the dynamics of angular shapes.

With some artists, the Dutch Piet Mondrian an extremest example, a subject in the true sense of the word was not present at all; the *composition* of the canvas became the subject matter with geometric and non-geometric shapes or "free" forms unlike recognizable objects. Such "non-objective" abstraction has only aesthetic satisfaction of well organized space, but it cannot be denied an important place in the status of modern art for modern architecture and industrial design have drawn heavily from this style which crosses lines at right angles to divide space into well related areas.

FUTURISM

With *Futurism,* a group of Italian artists just before the first World War broke away from painting their subjects as immobile objects. To approximate "time-in-space" they overlapped planes of an object several times in sequence. The concept was to effect movement in space as seen from the observer's stationary position. Giacomo Balla, for example, represented a "running" dog by painting the animal with many legs. Luigi Russolo's shape of a motor car superimposed with a series of directional angles, each more acute than the last, was an attempt to analyze the modern dynamic idea of *speed* by means of abstract lines and shapes.

Though not actually the work of a futurist, the "motion" in the multiple body of Marcel Duchamp's *Nude Descending a Staircase* is, perhaps, the masterpiece of this style in painting.

PURISM

Though equally short-lived, another derivation of Cubism carried abstraction to an opposite extreme. This is *Purism* inspired, as was Futurism, by the machine age. But while the Futurist was preoccupied with machines in motion, the Purist utilized straight lines and forms of machines at rest, recombining them in a design to reveal his imagination. Amedee Ozenfant

12 (Opposite) Another collage designed with plant material. This story telling scene is centered on nature with field grass arranged in its manner of growth and suggestion of habitat. The receding fence relies on linear perspective to suggest distance. An important factor is the pleasant relationship between negative areas (spaces) and positive shapes (solids). *Arranger: Mrs. Wm. Floyd Nichols— Photographer: John Hugelmeyer.*

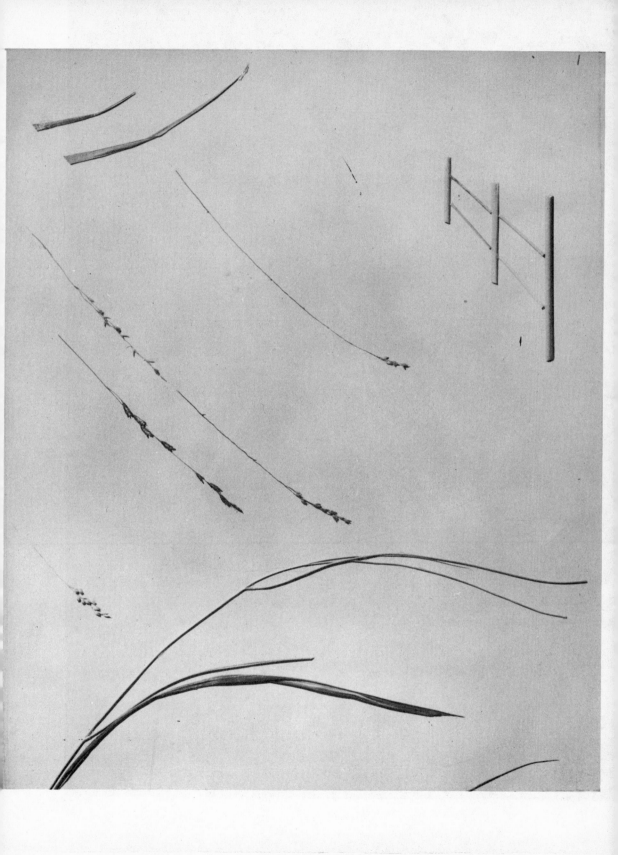

was a leader among the Purists. Plate 14 is an arranger's interpretation.

In modern design as in any structural art, fundamental principles are basic. In the abstractions we have discussed we find the principle of *contrast* emphasized—contrast not only in value, hue, texture, and shape, but in line as well. Spaces created betwen these opposing lines are not meaningless voids, but important areas of the design. To this day contrasting elements are distinguishing features of abstract art.

EXPRESSIONISM

But angularity is not a requirement in abstraction. Early in the twentieth century, even before the geometric quality of Cubism, *Expressionism,* propounded by post-Impressionists Van Gogh and Gauguin, was developing an abstraction which leaned towards a lyrical approach to design; more curvilinear and spiritual work was being produced. These artists, with their Expressionist contemporaries, were applying structural interest and color meaning to create a more personalized art. This doctrine raised an artist's expression of a personal emotion above subject matter in opposition to unemotional Impressionism which presented only a momentary sight, a surface reality. The post-Impressionists were the first to employ distortion for preconceived expression. Back in the sixteenth century, El Greco in Spain had indulged in a noticeable distortion of his figures, but it took the post-Impressionist artist to exploit it to convey emotional feeling. See the modern sculpture in Plate 15.

Van Gogh, for instance, dramatized perspective to suggest the confinement of the narrow room he occupied during his committment to an asylum. His passionate outbursts in such paintings as *Cypress Trees* and *The Starry Night,* revealed in swirling rhythms the imaginative, emotional, and spiritual world of the inner man, as opposed to the more orthodox tendency to record the world of outer man as practiced among his contemporaries. Plate 16.

Warm and cool hues were still important for achieving space il-

13 (Opposite) In this arrangement peeled grapevine is line which can be likened to that of the wire in wire sculpture. The shape made with it is like a drawing except that here, as in a wire‑sculpture, the line is in space instead of on the flat plane of a paper. Curled and spiralled, the branches give strong 3-D character to this linear construction. *Arranger: Mrs. Eric H. Feasy—Photographer: Russell Lawrence Young.*

14 Based on the straight line with the technique of a T-square and triangle, this non-objective design was inspired by *Purism,* an art style which employs precision, clean line, and the impersonal quality of machine design and engineering. Color (see dust cover) is forceful with the power of yellow in contrast to the blue carrying within them different tensions in advancing and retreating color. The brightness of the gourd functions as a sharp shock of color carefully placed in the grouping of muted color in the dried materials—wheat heads and stems, cut palm, banksia, lotus, and a split poinciana pod assembled on a series of bamboo mats. *Arranger: Mrs. Eric H. Feasy—Photographer: Russell Lawrence Young.*

15   Design holds solidly together with strong eye attraction in colorful croton and yellow chrysanthemums, and gladiolus leaves running to accord with the strength and elongation in the modern Madonna abstractly carved of Brazillian wood. Rock fragments on the right establish lateral balance. Space under the "bridge" stand makes this composition more powerful than were it flat with the surface of the table. *Arranger: Mrs. John M. Langenberger—Photographer: Dorn's.*

lusion, but they were now undeniably employed to express an *inner* feeling about an everyday world.

Gauguin in an assumed primitivism distorted shapes and painted them in flat exotic hues such as smoky violet and cerise. Placing a pattern made up of dark and light against the background absorbed him. A popular example is *The Spirit of Dead Watching*. This contrast he enjoyed so much is adapted to arrangement in Plate 17.

Gauguin was fond too of using unrealistic hues such as are shown in his pink sands and red dogs. Though distortion was dominant the shapes were decoratively delineated and the eye moves easily over his decorative patterns of harmonious color areas.

FAUVISM

In France a group of obscure young artists occupied a curious position in Expressionism. They were intrigued with Gauguin's colorful distortions. The grotesquely carved African Negro figures (see Plates 7, 8, 17) that later influenced

Picasso stirred their admiration too, and we find a primitive trait in the work of the Fauves. Their efforts, however, were so radical that in the 1905 exhibition their work was displayed together in one room nicknamed *Cage Aux Fauves* (wild beasts). And thus *Fauvism* was born.

In this movement intense and clashing hues were combined in unified composition— an "explosion of color" characterizes Fauvism. The leader of this group deeply inspired by Cezanne's architectural relationships was Henri Matisse, considered the greatest colorist in all modern art. Braque, Georges Roualt, and Andre Derain were among other artists associated with this short-lived movement.

Paul Klee, a German associated with the Fauves was a great proponent of the primitive, and was especially interested in learning how the relationship of content to structure was accomplished through instinctive Primitivism. He turned to the analysis of the simple direct drawings of children; such elementary beginnings affected his work which developed the style of

16 (Opposite) An arrangement inspired by the swirling rhythms of Van Gogh. Space flows around and also through this structure; it is measured but not checked by the plane of yellow celosia, dried castor bean foliage, pods of the century plant, and gray driftwood on a cypress slab. Solid pointed forms cut the space like a spear and the immobile seems to move—a reminder that design and expressiveness are more marks of the mind and hand than of subject matter. *Arranger: Mrs. Albert P. Micciche—Photographer: Bill Crenshaw.*

childlike art for which he is best known.

GERMAN EXPRESSIONISM

With Klee, the abstract painter, Vasily Kandinsky initiated *German* Expressionism. It is interesting that seeing Monet's *Haystacks* in 1895 was to him an event pregnant with possibilities for the future; a whole new attitude was born within him. So greatly impressed was he with the artist's expressive freedom that his desire to employ abstract representation in place of the traditional and natural rendition became an obsession. It was Kandinsky that suggested that abstract art be called *concrete* art for, he declared, nothing was less abstract than abstract art!

Early in the twentieth century Kandinsky's essay *From Point to Line to Plane* expanded the theory that all shapes can be abstracted into point, line, and plane. Plates 18, 19, 20. Color areas, he explained, fuse into high and low tonalities. Like Gauguin he employed color for its meaning. Leaving a recognizable subject out all together, Kandinsky, climaxed his theory a few years later in such work as his *Improvisation*. This was spontaneous and intuitive work which in itself was revolutionary, for canvases to date, except for some of the spontaneous ones of Van Gogh, had been carefully planned. It can be said that spontaneous painting came to a focus in Kandinsky. There is kinship in the theories of this Expressionist and the moderns of today with spontaneity a recognized value.

While the art of Chaim Soutine is too personalized to be linked with any one particular group, his distortions, hot hues, and richness of surfaces are in the spirit of German Expressionists. Plate 21 was inspired by the work of this "madcap Bohemian."

SURREALISM

At the close of World War I *Dadaism* was motivated by bitter revolt against the world in general. Dada was a destructive movement and so far as any lasting influential character is concerned, only the outgrowth of *Surrealism* was strong enough for our consideration.

Sigmund Freud, the Austrian founder of psychoanalysis, was a pertinent force. His popularized

17 (Opposite) On a slate-gray base which has been lightly brushed with gold and against a dove-gray velvet backdrop, velvety calla lillies with some opened to show the yellow spadix and other furled, metallic Rex begonia folliage, large black grapes with grayish bloom, and dried gray eucalyptus pods are combined for form and texture pattern. Forms are robust and composition is as simple and as solid as the forms all of which is in keeping with the African sculptures. *Arranger: Mrs. Raymond Russ Stoltz—Photographer: Boutrelle-Sevecke Assoc.*

18 A collective pattern of mass and line
directs the eye upward from a brass container which reflects the green of plant
material. Spacing (or timing) in placement of the onion flowers controls the
sight line. The eye is attracted to emphasis low in the design where it moves
slowly for spaces are somewhat closed,
moving more quickly when they open up
between the pause points of bloom
(these are interest areas), and stopping
in the round form at the top where the
eye is held momentarily, the dark green
foliage at the base finally pulling it
down to begin again an upward path.
Compare this visual track with that on
Plates 16 and 31 where pointed shapes
at the top tend to direct the eye on-
ward rather than arrest it. Comparatively more forceful element low in this
design is required to draw the eye back,
thereby keeping it within the arrangement as a means to unity. *Arranger: Mrs.
Forrest K. Bryan—Photographer: Curtis
Studio.*

19 A design based on nature's radiating pattern. The bright note of yellow in the Gloriosa daisy
(sunflower) is echoed in the higher and unopened blooms. However, the hue is not intensified
through contrast with dark brown toward the center as in the fully opened flower, and so the
higher blooms have less attraction for the eye, which is drawn first to the open bloom. The plane
of cattails has ascending direction to carry the eye upward where the partly opened flowers arrest
it momentarily, easing the eye's path back to the open sunflower to complete the cycle in this
unified composition. The dark brown modern container is textured pottery. *Arranger: Mrs. William
Wheeler—Photographer: William Wheeler*

20 Kandinsky's theory of abstracting elements into basic tangibles of point, line, plane, color, and texture (and we may add light and space), is easily recognized in this pyramidal design. Lotus in all stages of development is arranged in New Guinea black pottery on a series of black bases graduated in size. *Arranger: Mrs. Howard M. Oberlin—Photographer: Howard M. Oberlin.*

21   The strength and turbulence of a Chaim Soutine painting is expressed here by composing a vanished dishrag gourd and dried tan leaves of night blooming cereus against dark brown fabric which had been knotted to give it texture. You can see the forms as the arranger saw them. Can you feel what she felt in their combination? *Arranger: Mrs. Albert P. Micciche—Photographer: Bill Crenshaw.*

22 On a free-form black base strelitzia foliage, orange clivia flowers, small green bananas, and a
black figure from Haiti are combined into composition inspired surely by Dali's painted women
with bouquet heads. *Arranger: Mrs. Richard Warner—Photographer: Boutrelle-Sevecke Assoc.*

23 Like Plate 22 this arrangement, Surrealist is essence, creates strong imagery. The theme "reaching upward to the skies" is described by the arranger as follows: The container, a transformer for street electricity, reminds us that "we can be our own transformers, bringing our lives from sadness to joy." The crystal blocks represent the "skyscraper hopes of high ideals." The freshness of chrysanthemums is emblematic of the "always present life and hope," with the concentric circles, the "cycles of life." "Each individual starts life from the same level" is symbolized by the reversed base; the sponge represents "human pliability." *Arranger: Mrs. Edgar Littmann—Photographer: Eugene Taylor*

theories moved artists to express the fantasy of an imaginary dream world by placing unrelated objects in juxtaposition. This "ism" perhaps is best typified in the work of the Spanish Salvador Dali. His *Persistence of Memory* portraying distorted watches is one of the most familiar of these paintings which are dependent on strange and mysterious dream life for subject matter. To date Surrealism is the last major change in the art realm. Its greatest contribution to modern artists, and the layman as well, is that it opens the mind to impressions that help to break down indifference. Plates 22 and 23 illustrate Surrealistic traits in arrangement.

STRUCTURAL-EXPRESSIVENESS

Let us pause now and compare the trends which renounced academic style to develop art along freer lines. We find two paths parallelling the way toward stressing basic structure and ignoring surface representation of subject matter: the structural, architectural direction practiced by artists from Cezanne through Picasso to Mondrian, and the other road indicated by a sensitive use of color from Gauguin through Matisse to the spontaneous freedom of Kandinsky. Having traced the variety of interpretations which have kept modern art from becoming stereotyped, we distinguish two extreme forces underlying the production

of art in the modern movement. We discover that in the one, Abstraction, representative realism of objects or scenes is disregarded while in the second, Expressionism, we find abstract realism, a representation subordinated to emotional expressiveness. Though these two collective trends oppose each other, both are impelled by revolt against the restriction of traditional techniques—Abstraction by breaking through time-worn formulae, Expressionism by emphasizing accordance with self.

A blending of the two has activated a so-called *international style,* a synthesis of the abstract and the personal. This is *Structural-Expressiveness* which defines the most popular contemporary aspect of our generation. And rightly so, for in this merging we find pure abstraction modified by the relaxed lines and shapes characteristic of Expressionism, and the exaggerated emotional quality of Expressionism restrained by an attribute of abstraction. Art today has been completely liberated from traditional restrictions and has emerged as a new art style. Pleasing examples in arrangement are illustrated in Plates 24, 25.

MODERN RENAISSANCE IN AMERICA

In presenting the milestones in modern painting why has no reference to art in America been made? Fruitfulness of the modern movement in our country is reserved for

24 A driftwood "bird" on a sycamore stump
is the work of an arranger who is guided
but not dominated by her "problem"—a
narrow space beside a stone-ledge modern fireplace. With white-striped aspidistra, white fungus, echeveria rosettes,
and driftwood there is a three-plane
placement to supply depth. In relation
to the picture plane, the upright leaves
are parallel to the sides of the recess,
but those low in the design swerve forward with one spiralled in its swing
strengthening illusion of form. And at
the top, wood lies in planes thrusting
diagonally forward and backward. Arranger: Mrs. H. Henry Staley—Photographer: Boutrelle-Sevecke Assoc.

25 The spirit of speed and directness of our century is expressed in this "space ship"—a polished pine root diagonally supported on a cypress knee. Stripped of all non-essentials this composition presents the very essence of flight. Here is proof that abstraction in arrangement can be in the idiom of geometric form and still be personally expressive. *Arranger: Mrs. Robert Godley—Photographer: Mrs. Fred Langford.*

a separate analysis because until the late 1920s, London and Paris were the centers of art, and American artists thought it a must to study abroad. A significant practitioner is Mary Cassatt who was greatly influenced by the Impressionist methods of the French artists Degas and Monet, and by the purity of line in Japanese prints. Robert Henri strongly advocated self-expressiveness based on personal experiences. The whole theory of modern art is contained in his philosophy that the work of those who express themselves will never be outmoded.

Since the close of World War II American artists studying here at home have directed their efforts into a vigorous modern vein and today the city of New York is second to none in art production and influence. Among those whose work is most typical is Charles Burchfield. A resemblance to Van Gogh's technique of distortion for emotive impression is found in his paintings. By changing the natural shapes of things he created mood. An example is *The Night Wind,* a fantasy of mystery and eerie sensation. *New York Under Gaslight* by Stuart Davis is another well known American canvas that follows subjective expression. In this picture the spirit of the Gay Nineties is contrasted with skyscrapers of our day in an unnatural design of distortion and simplification based on the science of "time-in-space." This assumption that space

is continuous was, you will recall, a consideration of early abstractionists in Europe. Another modern of our day is Jackson Pollack who turned his back on nature and painted without any subject as in non-objective art of some of the European Cubists. His paintings might be said to be "records of movement" for he worked by moving his arm rhythmically above his canvas laid flat on the floor, and allowing the paint to drip and spatter from his brush. Results are pictures of rhythm and texture.

SCULPTURE AND ARCHITECTURE

Technique is a dominant difference between painting and the allied arts of sculpture and architecture. The painter deals with creating an illusion of space on a flat surface, the sculptor and architect deal with actual space. But in these arts revolutionary change parallels that found in painting.

SPACE IN SCULPTURE

Because of the nature of his medium and traditional relationship of sculpture to architecture, the sculptor utilizes architectural form and like the architect is conscious of space which supports his work; the atmosphere surrounding has become part of the sculpture.

It was the Romanian Constantin Brancusi who first brought new

26 An arrangement bold in color and shape with a balance of line against mass. A pattern of light
and dark as well as a rich color chord is developed. Materials are rose-pink celosia and yellow-
green strap foliage of amaryllis in a free-form black container. *Arranger: Mrs. Oral J. Jensen—
Photographer: Mr. Lon H. Thomas.*

direction to sculpture. His contribution of form simplified almost to abstraction is comparable with that of Cubism in painting. He has gained artistic fame with his slender, soaring, tapered marble or bronze forms in his *Bird in Space* sculptures. His abstract and symbolic work revealed a drive toward the simplified essence of a subject. Refer to Plate 25.

In the work of Jaques Lipchitz, also influenced by Cubists, the viewer is so aware of its existence in space that he is almost compelled to walk around it. In his early period the artist had little interest in subject matter; organic shapes, minus detail, were transformed into geometric form. Later he began to hollow openings in the mass for the penetration of light and space. This technique is illustrated in the container in Plate 26, and in arrangement in Plates 27, 28. From this he developed "openwork" forms or "transparents" as he called these skeletal sculptures of metal ribbons. The ribbon technique inspired the arrangement on Plate 29.

Perhaps the vanguard is England's Henry Moore, who is vitally concerned with space integration. His outdoor reclining figures, half rock, half human with huge limbs and small heads contain abstract and Surrealist elements.

Surrealism influenced sculpture to a great extent in calling attention to strange beauties in nature such as eroded stone, weathered wood, fantastic forms of tree roots, smooth-washed pebbles on the beach. The Surrealist movement also directed attention toward the way one form suggested another—thus the weathered tree root might with the aid of the imagination turn into a bird (Plate 30), and a bird might become a purely abstract form.

Moore is a direct descendant of Branscusi when it comes to appreciating a medium for its own sake. This concept led to experimentation with new materials such as aluminum and concrete.

Umberto Boccioni, a Futurist, tried to abstract the idea of motion within the static limitation of his medium with his *Unique Form of Continuity in Space,* a "moving" version, it is claimed, of the Grecian *Victory of Samothace.* An arranger abstracts the idea of flight in Plate 31.

Others, like Alexander Calder, a leading exponent in modern art in the United States, produced three-dimensional form which actually *did* move—the mobile constructed with wire, glass, and plastics. The relationship between shapes of material and shapes of spaces between make up a representational or an abstract design. Influenced by European abstractionists like Mondrian, Calder is dedicated to simplicity. His work makes no explicit claims and is often amusing— "a pure play of movement" based on the inherent joy of equilibrium. Plates 32, 33.

MODERN SCULPTURE IN AMERICA

In general, modern sculpture in

27 White amaryllis flowers with the foliage of sansevieria and philodendron present a balancing effect
of smooth texture against the rough of driftwood. The eye moves in and out and around this
arrangement as well as from side to side and from bottom to top thus creating a strong feeling of
deep space. *Arranger: Mrs. Henry Kirschenbaum—Photographer: Boutrelle-Sevecke Assoc.*

28 A distinctive quality of this arrangement of embryo palm and anthurium is the way all has been put in a spiralled tomion. Negative areas running throughout clearly delineate every shape and tone. Every area is without modulations which aids the simplicity of the design. A series of stands carries the eye in toward the subject increasing the impression of depth. *Arranger: Mrs. H. F. Dobbin —Photographer: Boutrelle-Sevecke Assoc.*

30   A pine root "eagle" sculptured by nature with Jerusalem oak (a weed) supplying height, and
     magnolia leaves, western thistles, small dried coconuts, and eucalyptus pods filled with green moss
     to add color, compose a design in earthy tones, rich in personal expressiveness. *Arranger: Mrs.
     Robert Godley—Photographer: Mrs. Fred Langford.*

29   (Opposite) Folding of palm foliage in this manner is entirely the arranger's own creation, not an
     echo of nature. Taking liberty with nature in the interest of design is the essence of modern art.
     A cluster of small green limes emphasizes the torch-like ginger freed in space. *Arranger: Mrs. Eric H.
     Feasy—Photographer: Russell Lawrence Young.*

31   Space is an important part of this stylized design to interpret *flight*. The scarlet of the amaryllis bud with the black coal at the base is forceful enough to pull the eye back from its thrust upward and sideward through the burned and cut palmetto (anything with a point directs the eye like an arrow). In this way unity, oneness of structure, is maintained. Croton leaves so dark as to be called black are touched with red. *Arranger: Mrs. Dorst Baumgartner — Photographer: Marvis Studio.*

32   (Opposite) This abstract mobile is the product of an imaginative artist who has discovered the thrill of creation. The "blossom" is made by whittling a maple stick at both ends; it is hung by a reed chain from driftwood which is anchored to a redwood base. This type is especially attractive under an electric lamp where heat thrown from it creates sufficient air currents to keep the mobile in continuous motion. *Arranger: Mrs. Henry B. Carter—Photographer: Andrew Bunn.*

33 Aware of the principle of balance and beautiful space relationships, this representational mobile is constructed by beginning with the bottom form and changing the balance point with each additional unit. The birds are hung by nylon fish line attached to each with a small fishing swivel allowing freedom of movement. The large bird is screwed in place; its immobility emphasizes the moving of the others. Birds are brown and orange; they are assembled from parts of plants. *Arranger: Mrs. James W. Riley, Jr.—Photographer: John Hugelmeyer.*

America takes advantage of the natural character of the medium with modeling, carving, casting, and welding directed toward symbolic abstraction rather than decoration or a narrative quality, and achieves a combination of material, form, and expressiveness to typify the most modern of contemporary sculpture. Use of new materials or new use of familiar materials are features of twentieth century sculptures. A case in point is the linear construction in space of the cage, Plate 34.

SPACE IN ARCHITECTURE

The conscious use of space inherent in modern sculpture is also found in contemporary architecture. Today a building is thought of more as an "organization of space" than as a mass of solid material. United States leads the world in modern building.

It is said that an American architect, Louis Sullivan, in 1890 gave the world the skyscraper, a structure with "movement" upward. His student, Frank Lloyd Wright, has

carried on and has placed emphasis on a prevailing geometric character. His attention is focused on function, spatial organization, exposed supports of attractive material (Plate 35), and use of the unadorned surfaces of new building materials for their decorative quality in color, texture, sparkle, opaqueness, or transparency (Plate 36). One need only refer to the extended use of metal and glass in architecture today to know that as in sculpture, new use of familiar materials has become a dominant feature in the modern trend.

ART IN THE FUTURE

In an attempt to understand modern art we are preparing ourselves for new styles to come. Further developments are a certainty, for all of history reveals that art is living and growing; without growth it would not exist. Already form and content are leaning toward a more individually subjective presentation. The urge to create in all fields of art is now a matter of conscious effort in the modern designer.

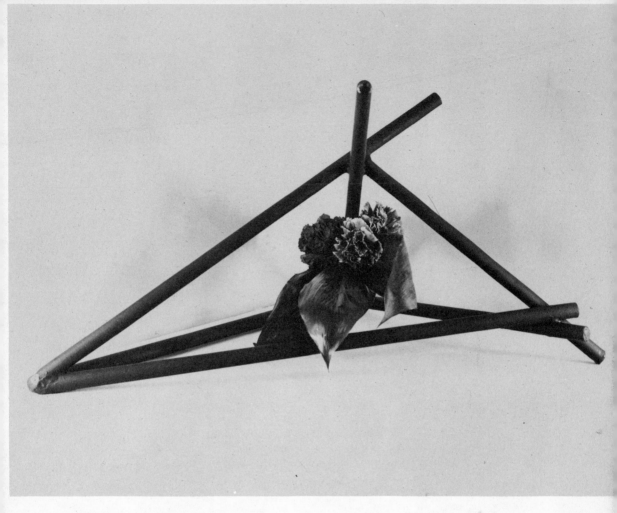

35 (Above) So modern this idea of composing plant material within an exposed frame of support. *Arranger: Mrs. W. Farnsworth Loomis—Photographer: John Hugelmeyer.*

34 (Left) A piece of contemporary craftmanship in fine white nylon string attached to a black wood frame furnishes an accessory in the modern vein—a cage, empty so that the viewer might conjure up his own idea of bird content. Such an abstract construction can be made by attaching the string (or wire) with U tacks hammered to a base. String can be tied at the top; wire can be twisted or joined together by means of an electric soldering iron. Materials are bronze-red and green canna and castor bean foliage, canna buds showing red, and a black plaque. *Arranger: Mrs. Jack Rardin— Photographer: Carpenter's Studio.*

36 (Left) The ceramic container, coral deepening at the base to mahogany hue, was made by the arranger. In it green foliage and anthuriums with coral spothes and yellow spadixes are arranged and staged in a flower show niche. Four pieces of light coral plexiglass (lighted from the top) cut the space to give dimension to the recess. Again we see that space is more important than mass in modern art. And by space eye direction is controlled. Here a series of sharp accents of the same hue pull the eye from one anthurium to another with a variety in spacing for more interesting rhythm. *Arranger: Mrs. Howard P. Serrell—Photographer: John Hugelmeyer.*

3

Contemporary
Arrangement Styles

Flower arrangement is undergoing changes similar to those found in all art fields. In the following pages we will attempt to describe the modern point of view in relation to this comparatively new art-form in America. Although we will pursue a discussion of concepts and not historical record, to recall preliminary stages is indispensable if we are to get the right perspective.

CRAFT OR ART?

Flower arrangement began in America as home decoration and arrangers were content to be artisans. Many still consider skilled craftsmanship the main issue. Be

that as it may, flower shows which have swept the country prove a growing percentage of arrangements are designed for the sheer joy of satisfying the creative urge, and the designer wants his work accepted on a par with fine art. If fine art is the aspiration, arrangers must take their stand with artists in other fields, and consider the age in which they are living. What yesterday was but arrangement intended to glorify the home interior, today is arrangement that is so very much more—a manifestation of creative art. As such it is subject to the flood of new ideas, new tastes, new standards that are emerging with changing attitudes, changing customs, and changing goals in social and industrial realms.

It is true that all this is nothing more than a foreshortened view of arrangers' attitudes, but it is also true that through understanding relation with the history of the times, we gain a better view of the artistic course of arrangement and the personal concept of arrangers. The vigorous and lively world of today is pulsating with opportunities for a freshness of technique for the alert and courageous arranger as the illustrations indicate.

TRADITIONAL AND MODERN STYLES

Since in creative arrangement there is so much more involved than skill no one person can prescribe a specific method as the only correct way to arrange plant material, for there is no one specific way, only numerous ways of carrying out individual conceptions. Once we allow a set formula to determine our procedure, an art style becomes stagnant, so let us keep in mind that each arrangement is a new adventure wherein the purpose for which it is intended is the factor that determines its style.

To clarify growth let us refer to the fact that like all art today, arrangement can be divided into two major schools, the *traditional* and the *modern*. The former practices representation, deriving its design from something that already exists. It is a literal picture of things as they are seen with the eye. The second deviates from the literal. It is a transcription whereby things are seen with *feeling*, so to speak.

Under both classifications, arrangements fall into two broad categories, the *decorative* and the *interpretive*. The purpose of decorative arrangement is to *adorn* a setting while the purpose of the interpretive design is to express an idea, a story, or a mood. The line between the two is flexible. In an arrangement primarily intended to decorate we may find an interpretive quality as well, while an arrangement intended to interpret a subject may also be decorative. Actually, if we gain aesthetic pleasure in designing and in viewing an arrangement, it matters little under which category we list it. It is only to broaden our understanding and to enable us to recognize possibilities that we make any attempt to differentiate. It is the most dominant characteristic that defines and determines the classification.

Each of these categories can be subdivided into two techniques. Decorative work can have a quality of naturalness, or a conventional approach, which we term *traditional*. Or the decorative arrangement can be *abstract* art which aims at the essence or innermost character of an object or an idea, rather than the naturalistic effect of conventional pattern.

DECORATIVE TRADITIONAL

Since the term "traditional" may mean different things to different

people we must come to some agreement of its implication in this text. As used here it is a general acceptance of customary practices from the past in rendering artistic work which still lives as a motivating inspiration.

In traditional arrangement plant materials are used in a natural manner so that they retain their physical identity. An honest likeness is the key, with flowers, for example, on their stems used upright in a manner of growth.

DECORATIVE ABSTRACT

In decorative abstract arrangement, the designer may have the same intent—that is, to beautify a setting—but he ignores naturalism and instead uses the plant materials purely as line, color, texture, and mass shapes arranged to give direction and rhythmical interval as illustrated in Plate 37.

Every arrangement is an abstraction to some extent for the materials when cut from the mother plant are abstract shapes employed as units in design. In other words, the plant materials are without subject. For instance, a chrysanthemum is nothing in itself; the flower has value only because of its color, its texture, its pattern, or its form.

As intended in this discussion abstraction means a degree removed from nature and not abstraction from it. The finished design is detachment from the literal or natural-reality as opposed to naturalness in the traditional pattern. To illustrate, let us consider this problem in relation to an interpretation of a bird. The arranger interested in abstraction doesn't try to make his arrangement of plant material look like a bird as the eye sees it. To his creative vision his subject is not a feathered winged creature but a form in flight, a symbol of freedom, or perhaps an impression of soaring height. See Plate 24 for personal interpretation.

The abstractionist arranger is concerned with simplification harking back to Cezanne's analysis of nature's skeleton into the cone, the cylinder, the sphere, or even further back to Kandinsky's attempt to break things down to point, line, plane, texture, and color. When an arrangement is devoted to abstraction, results are stylized. Things are arranged according to the judgment of the designer rather than in a conventional manner (Plate 38).

---

37 (Left) To design is to relate parts of a whole through repetition; variety, contrast, and balance. In this, the structure is deliberate and forceful. The dark green container with an overtone of rose is antique but how modern it looks! Dracaena leaves (rosy-hued and streaked with green) are fused into a single plane which provides a perfect background foil for the drama of the rolled leaves cradling maroon celosia. Contrasting textures heighten each other and the rolled foliage gives form to the whole. *Arranger: Mrs. F. Palmer Hart—Photographer: Boutrelle-Sevecke Assoc.*

COMPLETELY MODERN

Abstraction produces a truly modern arrangement. Physical reality in material and a naturalness of growth pattern is subordinated to, and is entirely replaced by *reality of character* in the "ultra-modern" examples. Pure design relationship between line, shape, form, color, texture, and space is of greater importance than the physical identity of the materials. In other words, the designer of a modern abstract arrangement uses familiar line, form, color, and texture of plant materials but arranges these in a manner not found in nature. The man-made shapes in Plate 39 illustrate this.

Almost anyone with training and perseverance can compose a fairly good decorative arrangement but more than skill goes into the abstract design. When we examine the abstract work among the illustrations, we see that there is first of all remarkable discrimination shown in selecting the component parts of the design. These are then combined with originality and a sensitiveness to the creator's personality.

OBJECTIVE INTERPRETATION

Like decorative arrangement, the interpretive is subdivided into two general techniques. On the one hand we have objective expression which is representational and thereby corresponds in its impersonal aspect to decorative traditional arrangement. In its primary purpose, that of conveying an idea, plant materials are arranged naturalistically. To interpret the sea, for example, an arranger will represent accurate details of a seascape—a shell, perhaps, combined with a massed design of blue flowers topped with white bloom to imitate the color of white-capped ocean waves. The finished product records a sight experience shared by all persons which renders it *impersonal*. In other words, it is without expression of a personal reaction to the sea. A *personal* interpretation, on the other hand, would make the viewer aware of the designer's personal feeling about the sea. Perhaps this might be conveyed by a weathered piling, a single large flower, and a lone sea bird accessory to make us feel with the creator the solitude of the sea. The former expression could transport you to the sea but in order to take part in the experience, you must concentrate on the arrangement, whereas the personal version by the juxtaposition of carefully selected parts gives you a *quality* of the sea itself, and this becomes a part of you, the viewer—there is no need to concentrate. This is subjective interpretation.

SUBJECTIVE INTERPRETATION

Subjective interpretation is truly

38 Pure form and line with materials used for decorative color, texture, and transparency are dominant factors and significant concept in this modern arrangement. Detachment from the traditional is highlighted by the long sweep of a gladiolus leaf under the sleek transparent container. Sword-shaped leaves and locust seed pods give "motion" to a static grouping of four onions. Nothing is extraneous, no false details intrude in this achievement. Arranger: Adeline E. Lyster—Photographer: F. J. Fischer, Veterans Administration Hospital, Madison, Wisconsin.

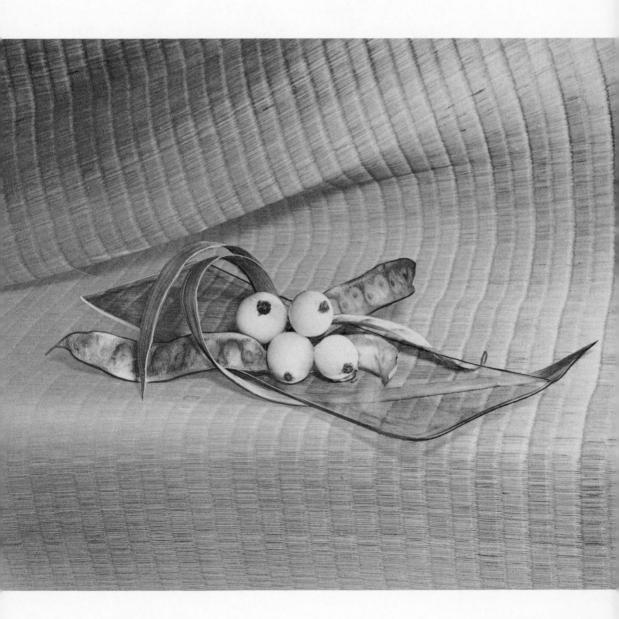

39 If modern abstract design is "taking apart and reassembling," this arrangement is most certainly in character. Beige colored "pansies" are made from conchs' egg shell cases, and ray-petaled "flowers" from a desert plant. These are combined with claw-like pods of Proboscidea or devil's claws tinted sea-green. *Arranger: Mrs. Robert Godley—Photographer: Mrs. Fred Langford.*

a modern aspect. It differs from the objective view in that the design's organization gives form to *feeling* rather than to vision, and so is personal. The arranger uses the same medium but composes shape, form, line, color, texture, and space to transmit how he feels about his chosen subject. He goes deeper than surface likeness and catches the spirit, character, or essence which to him is significant and hence worthy of emphasis in interpretation. In the personal reaction described above, the arranger would be expressing the inner reality as opposed to the outer or surface reality of the objective translation. An expression could be any one of many for each individual will react in his own unique way, a way that has been colored by his own individual-life experience.

OUTLINE FOR COMPARISON

I
TRADITIONAL
(Naturalistic)

1. traditional decorative is:
   conventional
   realistic
   prettified
2. objective interpretive:
   expresses the internal world
   is impersonal
   is representational
   gives illusion of reality
   is obvious
   gives form to vision

II
MODERN

1. abstract decorative is:
   expressive of innate
   character
   non-realistic
   forceful
2. subjective interpretive:
   expresses the internal world
   is non-representational
   is personal
   is subtle
   gives form to feeling

As has already been pointed out, it is as much a fallacy to say that the modern approach is the only way and to be more desired in arrangement, as it is to assume that the traditional way is the only way. One style cannot be said to be any better than another—it is simply a different problem handled in a different way and to be judged by different standards. Both schools, traditional and modern, have merit. The former is enjoyed because of the familiarity in the naturalistic; there is always a pleasant warmth and a feeling of security when we meet the familiar. On the other hand, the very lack of the familiar is the provocative note in the modern, for it is conducive to a much greater experience in audience participation. Both abstraction and subjective expressiveness demand of the viewer that he project himself into the art before him by insisting he experience his own judgment of the work. Examine each plate with this in mind. Does it make you think about the subject interpreted? Or about the artist? Or about yourself?

I must remind you that these styles can intermingle and more often than not they do as the plates disclose. But in every instance there is a style with definable emphasis that is just right for you. Be definite as to your *purpose* when arranging. Stand by the traditional or go modern; if you have no goal you will make little progress and will taste little success as a creative arranger.

4

Modern Japanese Arrangement

Just as artists of Japan have played a part in the evolution of modern art, modern artists have in turn influenced the arts of Japan. To properly appreciate this we must go back again into history. Early Impressionist painters, hungry for Japanese prints, focussed attention on Japanese art in general. To them the decorative character and delicate patterns were lessons in the value of eliminating the insignificant and in an awareness of an inherent beauty in things. Both are prominent traits in modern expression. Western artists painted what their eyes revealed to them; the Japanese expressed what they *felt* in relation to a subject in preference to what they *saw*, and with suppression of detail and simple and expressive contour lines conveyed *suggestion* rather than true surface likeness. This difference in technique was full of meaning for the early moderns.

In the building field Japan had always taken advantage of a natural beauty of materials in the simple homes of her people. A wood surface, for example, was hand-rubbed so the palm's oil was its sole treatment. Or grain was emphasized by removing soft portions of the wood leaving the hard fiber clearly defined.

America's most influential architect, Frank Lloyd Wright, admittedly delights in such appreciation of the natural in material and, too, in the Japanese all-purpose rooms with removable walls which open the home to lovely gardens. Without question, Japanese architecture has been a source of inspiration for modern building designs in today's world.

THE IKEBANA CULT

When Buddhism was introduced into Japan about the sixth century, it became the custom to offer flowers on religious altars. At first this was the concern of only the noble but later flower arrangement (Ikebana) became symbolic of a way of native life and has remained so through the centuries. A special alcove, the Tokonoma, to hold an arrangement for guests to admire, became a fixture in the home.

Until the turn of the last century the arrangements were designed according to rigid and complicated rules; only certain materials and certain containers were employed. In general these containers were higher than they were wide, and dark or grayed in tone to symbolize the earth. But around 1900, Unshin Ohara, a flower master, attracted notice by promoting the use of any container (even glass). Conditions were differing; foreign flowers were now being brought into the country and Ohara began to design containers suited to these

exotics. A consequence was a totally new type of receptacle, a flat shallow one, and a completely new style of arrangement. This was the *Moribana* with flowers and foliage used more abundantly to depict a natural setting of the woodland, a pond, a mountain view perhaps.

Here is a first break with Ikebana's traditional cult. Time-honored triangular structure and respect for natural growth and character of plant materials were retained, but the new method paved the way to more imaginative results. Today a variety of basic styles in the bowl or flat container (Moribana) and in the older vase (Nageire) are still popular among all schools of Japanese arrangement.

Since World War II the industrial age has changed life in Japan, and so too, the flower arrangements. Westernism has come into native homes and has freed the arrangement from the Tokonoma. Spiritual thinking of the Oriental, which had sprung from Confucian teaching that "man identifies himself with heaven and earth," has been modified to some degree with the more rational thinking of the Occidental. A blend of these opposing attitudes promoted a free-style art which beats with a new pulse in Japanese arrangement.

An opportunity for this new art spirit to gain strong foothold presented itself in early post-war days and was enthusiastically accepted. Wives of United States Army personnel at occupation headquarters in Japan availed themselves of study under the country's modern flower masters with the result that thousands of Americans today hold teaching credentials in the art of Japanese arranging; interest has spread near and far.

MODERN MASTERS

Sogetsu-ryu, a truly modern school, was founded in 1926 by Sofu Teshigahara, a master described by *Time* magazine (July 11, 1955) as the "Picasso of Flowers." Today he heads the modern trend among numerous schools developed from his instruction. Another stimulating teacher with the modern viewpoint is Houn Ohara, grandson of the originator of Moribana.

These moderns, and others, are today using anything at hand to work out the symbolic trinity of heaven, man, and earth in unrestricted proportions and placements in the design; such is left to the aesthetic judgment of the artist (Plate 40). Arrangements are conceived with plaster, iron, steel, wood (Plate 41), and sometimes are without any plant material at all. This drastic change, together with the new ideal that man should look ever forward and not be completely engulfed in past experiences produced what is known as a *non-realistic* school in contrast to the natural or realistic; growth aspect and inherent beauty are completely ignored. In accord with abstract art, this technique treats plant material simply as line, shape, form, color, and texture. In the most appealing examples emphasis is directed toward emotional impact—fear or elation, for instance. A piece of driftwood ceases to be driftwood and takes on meaning dependent on the circumstance, the designer, and the observer. Here is power to encourage the viewer to exercise his own judgment in relation to the artist's work. With this stronger audience participation, it is not surprising that the public is rapidly being introduced to a new art-style which one day will surely be every man's heritage.

DEBATE

In Japan today the controversy between those who defend the modern trend and those who passionately reject it is comparable to the one stirred up by early French Impressionism. Critics insist that just as Japan destroyed the sensitivity of their print designs by endeavoring to *Copy* Western techniques rather than adapt them, so too they are destroying their arrangement by accepting Western culture. It is true that we see work that has only novelty to distinguish it, with some examples completely at odds with beauty, even to the point of the ridiculous, but respectors of the new regard such designs as symptomatic of a growing art which, given time and

40 On a burl base, sand-blasted manzanita establishes the traditional three-dimensional form of a
Japanese arrangement in free-style technique. Graceful curves of wood are striking contrast to the
staright stems of yellow roses. Arranger: Mrs. Francis Leon Chrisman—Photographer: Boutrelle-
Sevecke Assoc.

41 A composition like welded sculpture to suggest the Sofu trend in Japanese arrangement. Materials are orange pods of Japanese lanterns, yellow-green peppers, Echeveria metalica, and dunewood. *Arranger: Zelda Wyatt Schulke—Photographer: Bryan Studio.*

chance, will emerge triumphant.

Arguments advanced against the "new look" in Japanese arrangements are to be expected. I have heard it said that "Ikebana has been robbed of its very soul," but this statement overlooks the fact that modern arranging allows the designer to develop his own ideas with a freedom which releases new potentialities. With discipline one learns to draw the line between the bizarre and the beautiful. Thus liberty is made subservient to self; first and foremost, self is satisfied. What is happening today in Japanese arrangement can be counted as contact between artist and viewer and a reflection of its increase. None can deny that this is wholesome growth.

THE TRIANGULAR FORM

The changes we have been considering are exemplified in the plates which illustrate this chapter. It is probable that not all will be acceptable to the reader for no two will always agree on merit or demerit in artistic expression. But surely everyone will agree that all show departure from the stereotyped arrangement of old-time Japanese technique, and are in themselves exciting contributions to the arrangement field.

Principal lines to establish height, breadth, and depth so typical of Japanese arrangement are traceable on analysis but in these free-style interpretations the lines do not always coincide with the fixed measurements of the standard patterns of the past. In every instance, however, they satisfy a first law of composition—unity within variety.

It is obvious too that all are in the triangular poise of the normal Japanese arrangement. In Plate 42 all placements are within the container rather than spread outward or forward as practiced in most Japanese styles. This is to accord with the name of the style, Heavenly, which inspired this design. In American arrangement a combination of the heavy with the delicate as is pictured here in the heaviness of the wood as compared with the lightness of the vine, would be avoided on the grounds of unharmonious character relationship. However, the vine gains importance and therefore "weight" through its unusual height and the way its pattern cuts the space at the top of the design, so that proportion and balance are aesthetically satisfying. Then too, since this was an arrangement in the Japanese manner, the "heavy" and the "light" respect a law of contrast for heightening effect which dominates all Japanese art. This law (In-Yo) makes use of negative and positive, passive and active forces symbolized by male and female elements—thin and thick, long and short, high and low, dark and light, etc. This canon of contrast accounts for the out of scale relationship seen in many Japanese arrangements in spite of their concern

42 Japanese three-line placement is set in free-style pattern by bittersweet vine, pruned for pleasing space intervals, and dark brown cypress wood. Supporting materials are hosta leaves and an unusual rock plant with violet stems and flowers. *Arranger: Mrs. Clifford E. Cyphers —Photographer: Boutrelle-Sevecke Assoc.*

for fitness of things.

Much of the charm of any arrangement comes from consideration of the size and shape of the space the design occupies, a sensitivity to distribution of light and dark, and the placing of elements to secure harmony and contrast. The work in Plate 43 by an understanding artist is no exception. While design here is largely the personal equation of the arranger, one recognizes suppression and restraint, techniques closely associated with old-style Japanese conventionality. Note the two cosmic forces, male and female, in light and dark areas, left and right curves.

In Plate 44, another beautiful display of modern work, free play is given to basic ideas endowing a realistic type of arrangement with a newness of spirit. How clear it is that every modern problem is contained within itself. Form and character are resolved by purpose, setting, and the nature of materials. And always a modifying factor is the nature of the arranger himself.

A prominent freedom in the design titled *He Laughs to See Such Sport* (Plate 45), pricks the conventional notion that even numbers are unlucky. Another liberty is one in the matter of scale. Traditionally, the Japanese measure size in this relation: To a mountain that is ten feet high, a tree is one foot, a horse one inch, and a man the "size of a bean." Because of this disregard for the traditional scale of the human figure in Japanese art, this arrangement may at first appear to be non-realistic in style, but the composition as a whole is designed not to be unrealistic, but to display the natural shape of plant forms so it must be classed as a free-style *realistic* type.

Just as some Japanese painters work for lively, even startling effects, and some for a quiet restful quality, so too the arrangers. Plate 46 uses plant material and container as symbols of an abstract idea. The work pictured in Plate 47 was planned as a forceful abstract composition — non-realistic in the full sense of the word. Inspiration came from the modern Sogetsu School, basic upright style, varia-

43 This masterful dried arrangement in Japanese free-style design was planned for a TV console against a gold-toned wall. The container is an incense burner (kere) of the Ming Dynasty. Plant materials are redbud and yellow daffodils. *Arranger: Eleanor Reed Bolton—Photographer: Albert Buquer.*

44 Inspired by the Japanese Nageire Senke School (over-the-cliff style), this arrangement was planned to show how well Japanese floral art fits our modern décor. Whether traditional or free-style, realistic or non-realistic, Japanese art is far closer to modern concept than the art of our own past. Candles, velvet-like in texture, were made by Mrs. Kenneth Barret. *Arranger: Mrs. Joe E. Wolff—Photographer: C. Fanders.*

tion No. 4. This is known as "Abbreviated Main Branch" style for only two of the usual three skeleton lines are employed. In respect for the basic law of contrast the high and the low (heaven and earth lines) are employed—only the auxiliary man line is omitted. In the standard pattern from which this particular work has been developed, depth is secured by earth swinging forward. In this mod-

45 Note the fantastic pattern of the height lines in this free-style realistic Japanese arrangement of
plant material is ignored; forms are considered only as shape, mass, color, texture, and direction.
material are humorous as well as beautiful." *Arranger: Kathryn Holley Seibel—Photographer:
William E. Seibel.*

ern interpretation, however, earth is regulated by the material and of necessity swings sideways. Lack of forward projection for achieving depth is compensated for by the filler material of berries arranged to direct the eye around to the rear thus supplying the depth dimension. In the non-realistic Japanese arrangement all units of the composition are carefully integrated so that form relationship is all important. For example, a container is not a container into which plant material is arranged but in the finished design it is considered as important an element as is the plant material. That the container might be employed in the light of just "another piece of plant material," the coconut spathe in our example was inserted in the spiralled wood to appear as a continuation of the weathered wood formation. Plant material is arranged on and around this "container" rather than in it. Though the calibash leaves are inserted in a more or less natural pattern they are glycerinized to a glossy jet black finish to satisfy the unnatural aspect of all plant material in the true non-realistic Japanese style.

46 (Left) Yellow chrysanthemums, star begonia foliage, brown cattails, and peeled wisteria in an earth-colored footed container combine originality and spatial concept into a design to interpret "Break the Sound Barrier." *Arranger: Mrs. Furman C. Horton—Photographer: Boutrelle-Sevecke Assoc.*

47 In this design inspired by modern Japanese non-realistic arrangement, the naturalistic character of plant material is ignored; forms are considered only as shape, mass, color, texture, and direction. *Arranger: Mrs. Clifford E. Cyphers—Photographer: Boutrelle-Sevecke Assoc.*

5

Modern Arrangements
in the Home

It is not surprising that flower arrangement, an art so closely associated with the home, should change as the dwelling itself changes. Let us consider what is happening today. The majority of American homes, even though they may not be modern in the full sense of the word, display the modern characteristic of simplicity in their structure and furnishings. Walls are broad unrelieved planes, and glass walls that just yesterday were a luxury item are now a familiar fixture. In general, homes are small compared to those of a past era with one room often serving as both living and dining areas. Partitions are avoided as much as possible to preserve continuity of interior space. Sliding doors or translucent Japanese shoji screens or just parallel rods do much to liberate space where divisions are particularly desired.

Space also figures prominently in our exciting new era of modern living when sliding glass doors or large glass windows open the home interior to the out-of-doors. The new dimension of light and space which comes with letting in the ever-changing charm of a garden view does away with a "closed-in" feeling.

LIGHTING AND EFFECTS

Interior decorators today recog-

nize the value of light in stressing form, texture, color, in drawing attention to specific locations, and in creating atmosphere. They are doing interesting things with light and light fittings, and the arranger is doing likewise. An example is the traditional pattern in Plate 48 brought up to date by a fresh approach through lighting. An arrangement is placed in such relation to the source of light that detail is lost and shadow cast on the plain wall space becomes the important feature.

Another type of arrangement particularly interesting where it can be lighted to throw shadow is the mobile. Refer to page 53.

While thinking of lighting I am reminded of the popular iron or brass floor lamp designed to hold a plant at the base of the stand. Home decorators will find it most effective when an arrangement replaces a plant. The combination of glass and metal is popular today in all home accessories; Plate 49 pictures such a combination with an arrangement.

CONTAINERS

A container is one of the major enrichments of arrangement; its selection cannot be a casual one. In unadorned geometric or freeform shape it reflects modern appreciation for simplicity. Many receptacles have openings (examples in Plates 26 and 29) allowing light and space to filter through their bodies thus emphasizing strong three-dimensional quality. Textured surfaces figure prominently.

There is no need to carry a discussion of suitable containers further since their essential character is so clearly seen in the illustrations.

ACCESSORIES

Quite analagous to the selection of container in developing a theme or plan is the choice of an accessory when one is desirable. Plate 50 takes a cue for its design from something other than container or plant material. Elegant and simple shapes of foliage and figure are combined with a continuity and appropriateness of design that has dash and drama. In the work in Plate 51 a true creative spirit has discarded formula and preconceived notion and employed a Madonna in a new manner of elegance. How assured we are that this arrangement takes place in deep space for the dimension of

48 (Left) Exploring new lighting effects, this arranger achieves a distinguished goal. The arrangement loses detail, becoming nothing more than a silhouette because it is lighted from the rear. But back light is supplemented by side light to cast the enchanting shadow on the plain wall and thus evoke a sense of depth. Materials in this "modern-traditional" arrangement are magnolia foliage and Fuji chrysanthemums in a globular bronze container. The figure is of wood, the base a teakwood burl. *Arranger: Mrs. Ernest E. Wunderly—Photographer: Edna I. Sander.*

49 A delicate precision is the keynote here. Solidity in the grouping of white gladiolus, its foliage, and green and white caladium leaves is a pleasant contrast with the emphasis on space in the container, an oval-shaped glass on a discarded metal electric light fixture; the preciseness in the plane of glass combines well with the metal—its curved bands echoed in the looped foliage. *Arranger: Mrs. Howard M. Oberlin—Photographer: Howard M. Oberlin.*

50 Color here is red-orange and blue-green. Both are somewhat grayed to weaken their forward and
backward tensions, but not enough to kill the drama of color contrast. The strong linear structure
of the blue-green aspidistra is supported in a tin can covered with copper paper, a good color and
texture with the red-orange drummer boy and base on which he stands. *Arranger: Mrs. Edward L.
Alexander—Photographer: William T. Radcliffe.*

depth is clearly seen. Clearly seen is an overlapping of elements and a "looking through to the rear"—two very real ways of achieving this desired sculptured effect. Other devices are as follows: gradation in size; contrast in size; atmospheric perspective; advancing and receding color; action that moves diagonally into the allotted space; position of container, accessory, plant materials, and arrangement as a whole in the space. For a detailed account see *Design and Depth in Flower Arrangement*, also published by Hearthside. It is devoted to three-dimensional arrangement.

A PICTURE INSPIRES

Whether the home that is begging for a new look is large or small, an arrangement to complement a modern painting can work wonders. The arranger whose work is shown in Plate 52 was intrigued by the organization and color of a modern oil. She found pleasure in the movement of simple radiating shapes, the design's dynamic thrusts, and the interplay of its contrasting hues.

Moderns are discovering anew the vast world of bold color in plant material akin to the forceful color that technical advances in dyes, paints, and fabrics offer the home decorator. When carefully selected and artfully combined, earthy, forceful, never wishy-washy color brightens our modern living.

Another modern picture inspired the arrangement in Plate 53. Its style here will satisfy the most discriminating taste and in color, texture, and simplicity of form structure, it is as new as tomorrow.

INSPIRED BY MOOD

In modern interiors, arrangements can create definite atmosphere to be changed at will. Plate 54 reveals such a plan. Designed for use on a Hi-Fi cabinet, the arranger attempted to express a musical mood. First a container to suit the interpretation of musical harmony was chosen—a modern version of a Japanese hand-drum. Curled branches and "notes" of white flowers were placed to create rhythm with a "chord" of light and dark adding to the design's smartness.

MEANINGFUL SPACE

Song of the Sea, Plate 55, gives

51 (Right) The dignity of this arrangement is particularly suitable where its simplicity of design will harmonize with an uncluttered modern interior. The composition was inspired by the lovely figure of the Virgin of Guadalupe, hand-carved by a native of Guadalajara, Mexico. *Arranger: Kathryn Holley Seibel—Photographer: William E. Seibel.*

52 Color is played here into a vibrant chord of pink, red, yellow, and green repeating the hues in
the modern painting. Black is introduced as a contrast element. Materials are anthurium and the
foliage of philodendron, sansevieria, croton, and clivia. The round-bottomed Indian jug is supported
in an iron tripod. *Arranger: Mrs. Johnson Stoddard—Photographer: John Hugelmeyer.*

pleasure of recognition rather than abstract speculation, so is primarily an objective expression; Plate 54 is subjective. But the use of space in the body of the arrangement is so distinctly modern as to warrant a place in this book.

It is attention to space that distinguishes the highly significant work on Plate 56 too. Each individual form is isolated in space to gain importance and results in almost primitive simplicity.

The matter of space is an abstract element to which many references have been made; it is definitely something to take into account. Though space is invisible it is at the same time perceptible for space areas are defined by the placement of solids.

MOVEMENT IN DESIGN

The creation of movement is an incentive to modern composition. Like a painting, an arrangement is without the time sequence present in music or dancing; it is a space art with all its parts seen at one time. But, as we know, placement of lines, shapes, and directions simulate a time element to give life and vitality to the immobile design.

Bright and lively rhythmic motion is expressed in *Hawaiian Memories* (Plate 57). The sensation is offered by the smooth and flowing driftwood to give the impression of graceful arms and hands of an Hawaiian dancer. Foliage intersects the spatial area

in varying proportions and directions adding emphasis to the intended mood.

SIMPLICITY

By concentrating on basic values of good design modern arrangers make a little material go a long way. Restraint is to be noted in a majority of the illustrations. By comparison Plate 57 has a wealth of material. But the artist makes each piece count in the design so that the finished product is strong in simplicity.

As a general thing this quality as applied to arrangement is misunderstood. Many believe it to mean the use of only a little material. In reality, simplicity is not necessarily omission. Rather it is an expression of a complex design or idea in a *direct manner*.

ADVENTURES IN DEFINED SPACE

To aid in creating mood a specially built recess is often provided, its shape contributing to the arrangement design. A simple case is a horizontal niche in the broad flat facing of the modern fireplace. Order implies a sense of direction in the design of the arrangement that goes into the niche, and direction takes its character from its setting, so a horizontal plan will seem to belong in such a place.

But an interpretive idea which might have guided the dimensions and location of a niche doesn't re-

53 A large pink flower of the dwarf banana, bold leaves of a variegated gray-green century plant
in a container of Swedish gray glass on a burnished silver footed tray combine into a clear-cut form
to complement the Chinese pictures. Note the beauty in the shapes of voids in this dramatic effect
staged on a space-saving nest of Chinese tables in natural teakwood washed with gray.
Arranger: Mrs. Albert Micciche—Photographer: Bill Crenshaw.

54 White roses, light green peeled wild honeysuckle with dark green Chinese holly (Ilex burfordi) in a plain container of white pottery produce an arrangement of strong modern character in its contrast of light and dark and its expressive content of a musical theme. Branches have been curled and submerged in water for a good soaking, and then dried in the sun to retain their shapes.
Arranger: Mrs. Oral J. Jensen—Photographer: Mr. Lon H. Thomas.

55 (Above) Integrated space is pleasing in a pattern of mass and void to interpret *Song of the Sea.*
There is agreeable pattern of color and pattern of light and shade as well. This arranger is not
afraid of texture; smoothness of glass fishnet floats enhances the rougher texture of dark curly kale.
According to the arranger of kale represents "wave tumbling over the silver-gray driftwood."
Other symbolism, she explains, is the "ocean's white-caps" in the white chrysanthemums, and "the
sunlight through the waves" in their yellow centers. *Arranger: Rae Pennington—Photographer: Lake
Oswego Studios.*

56 (Right) In a contemporary squarish bowl positioned to increase the sense of depth, a large cluster
of exotic seed pods of the Philippine lily, long green leaves from a serrated palm, large green
philodendron foliage, and curved bark are isolated in space giving drama and importance to each
unit and developing a structure of great simplicity. *Arranger: Mrs. Albert P. Micciche—Photographer:
Bill Crenshaw.*

quire monotonous repetition. The arranger can exercise considerable variety in designing her arrangement and still maintain unity whether her permanent space is defined by a special niche in geometric or free-form shape or by the placement of the furniture in the room. Achieve variety by working to bring together differing combinations of line, form, color, and texture with a change in emphasis— one time on line, another time on color, and still another on texture, and so on.

Of course the elements of line, form, shape, color, texture, space, and light do not exist alone. One may predominate but all are present in some degree and function together to control unity. We learn to use these interdependent elements by thinking of each one in relation to the others with which it will be seen.

So far as our medium is concerned to be modern simply means materials are used honestly for the sake of their own qualities. The elements of the design are selected not necessarily because they are plant material, container, or accessory, but because of significant relationship in a special situation. Forms act and react on each other developing a unified composition.

PLANT MATERIALS

For suitable plant material the modern arranger may choose from the fruits of man's horticultural triumphs or from among all the gifts nature places at his disposal. For him color, texture, and form are more varied and provocative than what is available to designers in other fields. In modern expressions, forceful form and bold or earthy color is preferred (Plate 58), but it is the effect through handling that is important. In Plate 59 a pale-hued feathery material is swept into simplified structure through magnificent restraint, with color and form subordinated to texture and tonality, and no one can deny it is modern in spirit.

TEXTURE CONTRASTS

This work is an illuminating example of pleasing contrast in textures — a contrast resolved into unity. The texture of the soft grass heads *absorbs* the light while that of the stems and figure *reflects* the light though it is muted to harmonize.

Few arrangers have discovered

57 (Right) Your sense of beauty responds to the richness of surface pattern in this arrangement titled *Hawaiian Memories*. It is constructed of green sago palm, cycas, strelitzia foliage, brown seed pods of anthurium, and a lei of pink and rose camellia flowers. Arranger: Mrs. Paul E. Cottrell— Photographer: Boutrelle-Sevecke Assoc.

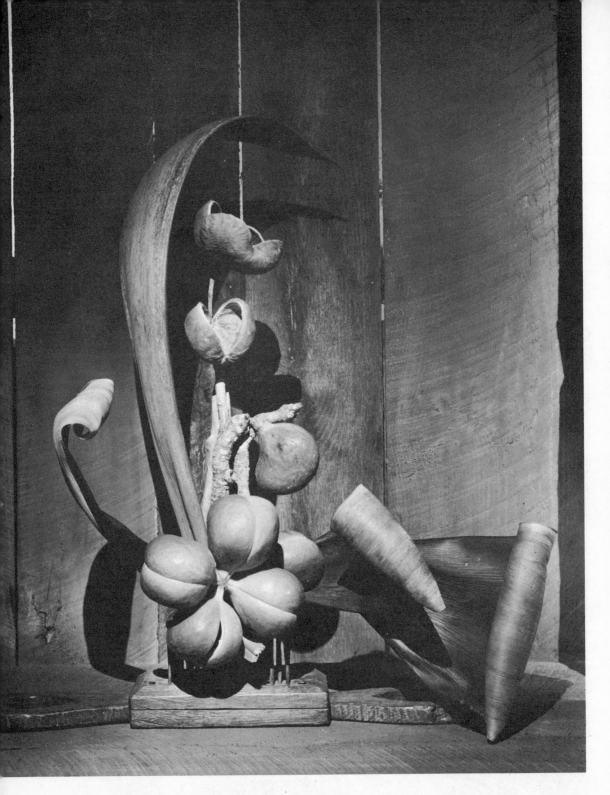

58 While consistent in underlying character the smoothness of bright red pods of Sterculia foetida
point up the rugged texture in the rough-barked stems and background boards. The container in
this powerful arrangement of startling forms was used originally to comb flax before weaving.
Arrangers: Mrs. Edward Duble and Mrs. Gertrud A. Mellon—Photographer: John Hugelmeyer.

the design possibilities with texture. The arrangements in Plates 60, 61 and 62, concentrate on texture in free modern individual interpretations.

In Plate 60 the smoothness of broom and wooden discs contrasts happily with the patterned feathers and flowers but in the arranger's own words, "only a little of the contrasting material was used to keep the pattern free and delicate."

Plate 61 is an especially fine example of the modern use of *sparkle*. Fashion has discovered how glamorous a *little* gleam can be. We find veins of metallic threads woven into drapery and upholstery fabrics. Actual metal chips are imbedded in floor coverings. Legs or strips of metal on furniture illuminate a whole new concept in home furnishings. As light reveals this arrangement (Plate 61), the plastic wheat sparkles, presenting an old pattern renewed through new material—the result is "modern-traditional."

The inner freedom of the artist, perhaps the most valuable attainment in modern art, is especially apparent in Plate 62. Contrast exists not only in texture, but in line, in angles, and between straight shapes and curved. In fact, it is the forceful variety of contrast that prevents monotony of an obvious repetition in this simple balance of symmetry.

In examining these examples we are led to say that they are illustrative of "harmonized contrast." It is true indeed that in all aesthet-ically rewarding composition, harmony and contrast are both required.

THE MODERN LINE

Do not pass by this last intriguing arrangement without pausing to study all details. Let us look to the dominant line pattern of the strelitzia. One might call it the *modern* line of beauty. In the eighteenth century England's William Hogarth focussed attention on the winding curve of an elongated S as a "line of beauty." Moderns in this twentieth century can still appreciate the grace and balance of this line influenced by Rococo art, a preference of the age in which this artist lived, but it is without strength or tension so important to modern viewpoint. The strelitzia line follows the path of a short curve with a long straight or almost straight line—a line of grace but with force and tension as well. The straighter the line the greater the tension, representing potentiality for endless movement. It is as though for this flower form nature had borrowed the contour of bodies that most perfectly adapt themselves to the flow of water and the current of air, the fish and the bird. Such is expressive of movement which is man's great interest today; we see it everywhere in many familiar objects.

BALANCE

It is of value to note the well

59 Dignity and delicacy are united here in an imaginative modern arrangement. Color plays a minor role—pattern is the thing. Note the similarity of pattern in the grass to that in the mane and tail of the horse. Because size and shape of the areas differ the repetition intensifies the theme rather than takes from it as might happen were areas of repeated pattern completely unvaried. *Arranger: Mrs. H. Henry Staley—Photographer: Boutrelle-Sevecke Assoc.*

60 Here a modern designer, using what was available, developed a thoughtful and ingenious pattern of repeated shapes and contrasted textures. *Arranger: Mrs. Eric H. Feasy—Photographer: Russell Lawrence Young.*

controlled time sequence in this arrangement for it proves that the symmetrically balanced design is not necessarily without rhythmic vitality. It is only the monotonous and unimaginative rigid "formality" apparent in so many symmetrical patterns that tags this type of balance static. Balance doesn't mean repose in the sense of inaction; it means that active force holds other active force in equilibrium. The problem of conspicuous areas (such as the elevated blooms in Plate 62) is one of the most difficult things to cope with in balance. Stability in this arrangement is due to an equality of eye attraction between the color and interesting surface pattern in the foliage area and the color and intricate form in the two strelitzia blooms. As a result all details are seen simultaneously. Actually, the eye moves from interest area to interest area but as it is drawn to one part of the composition it remains aware of all the rest of the design which we know is paramount. Through good balance and well-controlled rhythm, details are continuously related to the whole so that the arrangement is seen at a glance as it were. In other words, the collective pattern of intervals in shapes, lines, and spaces produces an eye path of direction achieving unity.

The principles of balance and rhythm are very closely allied for shapes and lines move in one direction or another, and it is balance that keeps the "moving" areas in equilibrium.

The balancing of movement is the distinctive note in the work on Plate 63. The eye passage in the design moves from the lower right diagonally toward the upper left. The arranger's problem was to control the eye in its course along the diagonal so that it could return easily to begin the experience anew. The open pattern of the driftwood at the base has enough pull on the eye to do just this.

THE SITE AFFECTS DESIGN

What is kept uppermost in our mind as we study these arrangements is the fact that they take their character from their purpose with their settings showing them off to best advantage. A prescribed setting guides the arranger in creating an appropriate atmosphere, in emphasizing mood or associations, and in revealing the structural beauty of the plant material.

At this point let us dwell a moment on proportion which refers to relationship between the parts and the whole. In itself proportion is nothing—it is entirely a matter of

61 (Left) An arrangement proving elegance need not be extravagant. In a contemporary ceramic compote are fruit, vegetables, and pine sprayed with white paint, some very lightly to give a transparent effect harmonious with the plastic wheat. On a pedestal the arrangement is as "special" as a staged museum sculpture. A dominantly white arrangement admirably fits the trend for white rooms. Arranger: Mrs. Raymond Russ Stoltz—Photographer: Boutrelle-Sevecke Assoc.

relation to environment. Good proportion means not only that the parts are related in size to each other but to the whole and *in a way that is desirable for a particular purpose or situation*. This is why we must think in terms of the shape of the space that frames the entire design, and of equal importance, the space of the room in which the arrangement serves as decoration.

In a small low-ceilinged room a tall narrow arrangement can in effect raise the ceiling thereby, through optical illusion, increasing the feeling of space. Plate 64 is an example.

Knowing that there is nothing like a mass of color to make a room look rich and festive in quiet good taste, the arranger concentrated on well related planes of color on all sides of her design achieving structural depth, a quality too often neglected in tall narrow compositions. She developed a columnar form by turning gladiolus to the rear and to each side as well as facing them toward the spectator. Such a plan is congenial not only to a tall narrow space, but to a

position before a mirror. Or on the floor beside a free-standing staircase designed to keep today's interiors spacious, a very tall arrangement does much to soften this functional area.

The arrangements in Plates 65 and 66 are planned to be looked down upon. These are compatible with the vogue of "low-level" furniture that is being introduced more and more into American homes. The "down-low" trend reflects a Japanese influence on interior decorating and gives a greater sense of space in our small informal rooms.

In Plate 65 perhaps it is the simplicity through the use of forceful material in a restrained pattern that is the outstanding character; there is calm quiet beauty in every line.

The work in Plate 66 was designed for a large low coffee table. The selection of plant material which is seen to best advantage when it is looked into—in this instance, beautifully veined and textured Savoy cabbage—adds to the charm of an arrangement in this location. And in deliberately re-

62 (Left) No filler materials are used between the area of foliage and flowers so each unit had to be carefully controlled. Only necessary elements were employed in grouping plant material into a straight vertical direction to contrast the spiralled rhythm of the iron band (from a piece of heavy machinery) coiled around a painted tin container. The base is black cement. An especially wise choice of plant material is the croton foliage which gives pattern and at the same time repeats some of the color in the strelitzia blooms. Their stems importantly bear the same thickness as the iron coil. *Arranger: Mrs. Margaret M. Claucas—Photographer: John Hugelmeyer.*

63　In contrast to the rigid symmetry shown on Plate 62, here is relaxed asymmetrical balance. Line can be restful or active as it is in this diagonal pattern composed of orchids, dracaena and iris foliage. When the oblique line rather than moving into space, parallels the picture plane as it does here, it may be unstable and require anchorage. The driftwood at the base supplies a counter force for stability in this design. *Arranger: Margaret D. Grumbine—Photographer: Boutrelle-Sevecke Assoc.*

64 There is calm quiet in this columnar arrangement of architectural precision, imposing against a pinkish-beige wall. Intervals of light and dark give pattern to this grouping of pink gladiolus and canna leaves in an amethyst glass container. Extreme height adds a modern look. Rolled leaves at the base stabilize. *Arranger: Mrs. Forrest K. Bryan—Photographer: Blick's Studio.*

65 In using as few lines as possible the designer has created an arrangement in keeping with the unadorned surfaces of a modern home interior. A pale yellow flower of the swamp caladium gives height. Curved green pods are from the same plant. Green leaves at the base are from the orchid tree. The container is dark green. *Arranger: Mrs. Albert P. Micciche—Photographer: Bill Crenshaw.*

versing some of the sunflower centers, the arranger induces the observer to look at the other side of the composition.

In discussing these arrangement adventures suited to modern American homes, one is conscious of a great diversity in original techniques. Let us remember that the creators have not gone out of their way to be different; they are simply individuals who see differently, and feel differently, and arrange with freedom.

66 Distinguished work depends not upon extravagant material but upon an understanding use of what is available—in this case, Savoy cabbage and spent heads of sunflowers. Here in a design for a large low coffee table, directional placement of the elements encourages the eye to move easily over the surface of the composition and around it. This is accomplished by turning some material toward the light, some away from it, and by reversing some of the sunflowers. *Arranger: Mrs. Henry Bircher—Photographer: Howard M. Oberlin.*

6

A Parting Word

It is now time to recapitulate. Modern art is anything but repititive; the many influences have made a particular style impossible. For the illustration of modern concepts the foregoing plates and text reveal a great diversity in type. Examples ranging all the way from the "modern-traditional" to the "non-objective" offer a seeming incongruity of approaches and yet in each instance, order and direction in the new techniques, the new aspects, point toward one main goal—to pursue arrangement not for its own end which has previously been a practice, but to de-velop one's own ideas and so, one's self.

The modern arranger has an eye for the structural character of his medium and has learned to think in terms of color, texture, shape, and line. He exploits the potentialities of simplicity, of contrast, and of space, and reveals a portrait of his own personality.

What does all this add up to? This: American flower arrangement is an expanding and a growing art form. Its very transitory character should be enough to free arrangers from bonds of conformity, but there are still those who like to play safe by designing according to traditional concepts,

117

thus losing harmony with a changing world.

Arguments against an over-emphasis of the new freedom in designing are advanced by some on the grounds that it will discourage the inexperienced from accepting arrangement as one of the fine arts. *But this is not the case.* Despite what at the present time is a comparatively small group of followers in modern tendency, the new impetus toward change in arangement steadily gains disciples to whom freedom is fervent challenge. We can count it a particularly happy sign that not only are more and more experts succumbing, but also beginners, and indeed the latter in particular!

must test for yourself. Do this by challenging every arrangement to decide in your mind just why a composition gives certain effects. Ask yourself:

Is there repetition to arrest attention, making one idea dominant?

Is there enough variety to maintain your interest?

Is the arrangement suited to its purpose? Its setting?

Do accessories contribute something to the whole?

Is there continuity of an easy eye passage with parts emphasized in proportion to their importance and intended function, and forces carefully balanced so that the whole has unity?

SELF DISCIPLINE

Creative faculty in modern arranging is developed by *doing;* the more it is exercised, the more imaginative quality you will find you possess. Be willing to be different; unusual solutions are often the best and certainly the most fun to work out. But there is need of self-discipline within a technical freedom, and the greater the artist's freedom, the greater must be his discipline. Just as some old ideas may be always good, some new may be undesirable. Develop critical ability. Do not accept everything you hear or read without thought and reason. You may obtain opinions from others but in the end you

THE FINAL TEST

The final test of any good composition is to view it upside down to better study relationships; freed from the subject matter, shapes emerge more clearly.

One cannot deny that modern arrangement is nourished by the past but it grows out of contemporary experience. To be successful the arranger must understand its development and be able to discern essentials that reflect our modern spirit both aesthetically and practically. Perhaps the most prevalent is the right to experiment. In other words, if the arranger will hold on to the best of what has already been achieved, and if he will add something of what he has explored and learned for himself, the result may well be a worthy success. And more important, it will suggest that there is discovery still to be made; an adventuresome attitude acknowledges a continuous need for improvement.

A PARTING WORD

I predict that the new-found freedom in designing will remain constant stimulant to arrangers, though at this writing it is just beginning. But a beginning, like a seed, needs attention if its growth potentialities are to be realized. It was with this in mind that I attempted this book. Although plates and text may hold no more than a cross-section of modern arrangement, it is hoped that they will offer a sort of working procedure in present-day arranging which promises to be the finest period thus far in the history of the art. If my desire to stimulate thought is fulfilled I will not care whether or not I am agreed with completely, for I will have contributed to a consideration of the subject of modern art in arrangement. With this I am content.

Let us honor what has been done in the illustrations, and anticipate with excitement future development.

Index

Cyphers, E.H.
  Modern art in flower arrange-
ment.   cop. 2